IMAGES
of America

CAMP MA-KA-JA-WAN

Eagle Scout Draws Map of Camp

The above map was drawn by Eagle Scout George Bersch, one of the outstanding Scouts of the North Shore Council. He is 19 years old and has serv on the Ma-KKa-Ja-Wan staff for the past two years. The aerial view of Ma-Ka-Ja-Wan is accurately portrayed in the above map depicting every ir portain detail in Camp.

This map of Camp Ma-Ka-Ja-Wan was drawn in 1931 by staff member George Bersch. (Courtesy of the Bersch family.)

ON THE COVER: Scouts pose on the dock with a sailboat at East Aquatics around 1952. Wally Trezise is sitting on the dock, nearest the photographer. Larry Smith is to his right. (Courtesy of Hank Jostock.)

IMAGES
of America

Camp Ma-Ka-Ja-Wan

Ian Hopkins and Matt Horbal
with an introduction by Jim Neubaum

ARCADIA
PUBLISHING

ISBN 978-0-7385-9890-1

Published by Arcadia Publishing
Charleston, South Carolina

Printed in the United States of America

Library of Congress Control Number: 2012950170

For all general information, please contact Arcadia Publishing:
Telephone 843-853-2070
Fax 843-853-0044
E-mail sales@arcadiapublishing.com
For customer service and orders:
Toll-Free 1-888-313-2665

Visit us on the Internet at www.arcadiapublishing.com

Dedicated to the Scouts of Ma-Ka-Ja-Wan you've heard so much about.

Contents

ACKNOWLEDGMENTS

During the past decade, a steering committee comprised of former and present camp staff members has researched the history of Camp Ma-Ka-Ja-Wan and unearthed much of its past. This book is the product of those labors.

Many contributors assisted in researching and writing the chapters of this book. It was a true team effort. Each person came to the table with the spirit of Camp Ma-Ka-Ja-Wan in their hearts. The contributors include the following individuals: Kevin Baldwin, James L. Chandler, John Hopkins, Joe Jordan, Paul Jordan, Robert G. King, John Lillstrom, Jim Neubaum, Steve Silca, and Barbara Ziegenweide.

Special thanks are due to Mrs. Wayne Dalton, a cook in the 1940s, 1950s, and 1960s, whose contribution of postcards from 1947 set this project in motion. Special thanks are also due to Patricia L. Girtz of Pearson, Wisconsin, for her long involvement with Camp Ma-Ka-Ja-Wan and her passion for local history.

Compiling a history spanning over 85 years requires input from dozens of people from several generations. It is impossible to thank everyone who has contributed to Ma-Ka-Ja-Wan's history, to CampMakajawan.org, or to this project directly over the years, but we are indebted to each and every one of them. This project could not have happened without their help.

Ian and Matt wish to thank their families for their patience and continued support throughout this project.

Author royalties from this project will benefit Camp Ma-Ka-Ja-Wan.

Unless otherwise noted, all images appear courtesy of the Northeast Illinois Council, Boy Scouts of America (BSA).

Introduction

The founders of Camp Ma-Ka-Ja-Wan had a vision of finding a location for a summer camp for the young people of the North Shore Area Council, BSA. The organizers sought to provide an outdoor experience that youth could not achieve in their home area, as well as a location with ample land on which to expand.

The first Scout executive, Walter MacPeek, was assigned the task of locating a site. MacPeek spent 10 days searching around Rhinelander, Wisconsin. Failing to find what he wanted, a chance meeting at the Elcho Inn with a Winnetkan who had an interest in the Thunder Lake Lumber Co. brought the suggestion of land near Pearson, Wisconsin, as a site. With major gifts from General Wood and Albert P. Snite, the purchase from Walter J. Hammond and the C.W. Fish Lumber Company was made possible. The foresight of these men led to buying the land surrounding the lake, so that the original 240 acres of the present East Camp at Ma-Ka-Ja-Wan was increased to 450 acres within a few years.

The founders' dream of purchasing their own summer camp was fulfilled on July 26, 1928, under the leadership of Walter MacPeek. The location was exactly what they were looking for and more.

Since its conception, Camp Ma-Ka-Ja-Wan has become one of the North Shore Area Council's, and, later, the Northeast Illinois Council's, finest and biggest assets. It has provided countless young people, adult leaders, and their families with an opportunity to enjoy the Northwoods of Wisconsin. By attending Camp Ma-Ka-Ja-Wan, all participants were given the opportunity to learn Scout skills, develop leadership skills, grow as individuals, and establish long-lasting friendships.

Throughout the past 84 years, numerous individuals have served on the Camp Ma-Ka-Ja-Wan staff. They brought with them enthusiasm, commitment to the high ideals of Scouting, and love for the outdoors. They also have had a big influence on the lives of the many young people who attended summer camp. One of the byproducts of being on the camp staff was to experience the spirit of Ma-Ka-Ja-Wan. That experience is something that many will carry for the rest of their lives and that many have already passed on to future generations.

As the years have passed, Camp Ma-Ka-Ja-Wan has updated its programs and continued to serve young people from the North Shore Area Council, BSA. In the early 1970s, with the merger of three area councils, the council's name was changed to the Northeast Illinois Council. With the expansion of the camp to over 1,500 acres, the name was changed from Camp Ma-Ka-Ja-Wan to Ma-Ka-Ja-Wan Scout Reservation. Camp Ma-Ka-Ja-Wan now includes East Camp, West Camp, Camp Wabaningo, a High Adventure base, Triangle M horse ranch, and a maintenance facility.

In the advent of low impact camping and changes in the types of programs available to the youth of the Boy Scouts of America, there were additional programs added to Ma-Ka-Ja-Wan Scout Reservation's outdoor plan. They include Porcupine Mountain backpacking trips, raft trips, canoe trips on the Flambeau Flowage, sailing on Lake Superior, and additional High Adventure Treks.

This book documents the personal stories and milestones of Ma-Ka-Ja-Wan Scout Reservation. It also tells about the vision that the staff, volunteers, and local residents had when it came to the summer camp. It is important to preserve the history of Ma-Ka-Ja-Wan Scout Reservation, so it can be shared with future generations. It will be the legacy of the founders of Ma-Ka-Ja-Wan and others to build on.

We hope that this book serves as a vehicle to promote more investigation into the history of Ma-Ka-Ja-Wan Scout Reservation. Possibly, we might hear more stories about Ma-Ka-Ja-Wan and unearth new historical photos from our Scouting friends. They might tell even more about the people who built the structures at Camp, and who developed a plan for the program.

As you look through the pages of this book, keep in mind the historical items you know about your family, church, school, and so forth. There's going to be something that you have learned along the way, something you can pass onto future generations.

Within the past 84 years, there have been many milestones for Ma-Ka-Ja-Wan Scout Reservation. Some have been documented, but there are many more to be shared. To compile this book, the authors and contributors went through thousands of photos, articles, and interviews. There were many more things to cover, but they might emerge in future editions of the Camp Ma-Ka-Ja-Wan book series.

Finally, on behalf of the Northeast Illinois Council, BSA, I would like to thank you for your purchase of *Camp Ma-Ka-Ja-Wan*. We hope you will enjoy its contents and how Ma-Ka-Ja-Wan has had an impact on the lives of many young people, adult leaders, and families.

—Jim Neubaum, Reservation Director

One

The Early Years

Ian Hopkins

Camp Ma-Ka-Ja-Wan has been part of the Northeast Illinois Council BSA's outdoor program since the summer of 1929. It has a rich history and has touched the lives of countless young people and adult leaders. The early history of Camp Ma-Ka-Ja-Wan is best described in the booklet "Scouting grew a boy, a man, a program, an ideal, and action, 40 years 1927–1967, North Shore Area Council, B.S.A."

At the turn of the 20th century, the 1,560 acres making up Camp Ma-Ka-Ja-Wan was covered by a growth of virgin pine. Many of these giants of the forest measured three to four feet at the base and towered 125 feet into the sky. By 1910, this virgin forest fell to the lumberman's axe. The tangle of slash, tops, and limbs created a fire hazard, and for the next 20 years, sporadic forest fires broke out in this area, burning the land.

The pine was replaced with a second growth, largely of hardwoods—maple, oak, and, of course, poplar. Lake Killian's clear waters teemed with walleye pike, northern pike, black bass, and pan fish. It was a popular fishing spot for local residents. Burnam Skidmore farmed a few acres at the northwest end of the lake.

In 1928, Walter MacPeek, the first scout executive of the North Shore Area Council, learned of this location. Early in July 1928, a committee composed of Frank S. Wichman of Highland Park, Charles A. Steele of Glencoe, George Walkley, and Jay Lightbody made a weekend trip to the area to look it over as a possible summer camp for the council. They were thrilled with the beautiful lake and its sand bottom (perfect for good swimming), and the potential for the second-growth forest crop.

These photographs, taken from the middle of Lake Killian in 1931 (above) and 1947 (below), show much of the original purchase that was concluded in the fall of 1928. It comprised about 240 acres and included the northeast end of the lake and the northwest end, comprising the Skidmore farm. The early committee displayed great foresight, realizing that complete control of the lake was essential to the future development of the camp. Thus, within a few years, additional purchases of land, including the resort at the south end of the lake, gave complete control of Lake Killian to the committee, with total ownership of around 450 acres.

Under the leadership of Scout Executive Walter MacPeek, the Camping Committee developed a plan for a summer camp. It was decided to erect numerous buildings to prepare for the grand opening of the camp in the summer of 1929. Among the structures built were a dining hall, camp office, waterfront boathouse, icehouse, and many other buildings.

On the 240 acres, campsites were cleared out, like the one pictured here close to the dining hall and camp office. The primitive campsites had no running water and used simple latrines and washstands. At that time, the camp used wall tents, as is the case today. A tent housed two Boy Scouts and was placed on a wooden platform.

The Scouts who attended in the early years would take a train to Elcho, Wisconsin, from Highland Park, Illinois. After arriving in Elcho, they would stand in the back of a stake truck for the trip to the west side of Spring Lake. The Scouts would unload their gear and place it in a large US Navy barge, which would take it across to the barge dock on the east shore of Spring Lake, which would later be unofficially renamed Lake Killian.

The barge and its 90-horsepower outboard motor were operated by a barge tender. The tender would be called to either side of the lake by the ringing of a large bell. The barge was also used for transporting food and equipment across the lake until the construction of the road around the south end of the lake. Wally Peterson (shown here) was one of the barge tenders in the 1940s. (Courtesy of the Peterson family.)

One of the few known photographs of the barge is taken from a 1947 postcard. According to Ambrose Cantagallo, there were several barges through the years. All were disposed of by sinking off the East Camp Firebowl. Greg Jones, a staff member in the 1970s, has since dove the site to examine the remnants. He has reported that there was not much left. (Courtesy of Ruby Dalton.)

While the camp was closed during the off-season, many of the local residents and adult leaders from the council would fish Spring Lake. Adult leaders from the council would come up to cut ice out of the lake in winter to provide refrigeration during the summer. This volunteer group worked with Caretaker Burnam Skidmore, who took care of the camp year-round.

This building, later known as Sherwood Forest, was one of the oldest at camp. Constructed to be the first health lodge, it was located on the road going down to the East Camp office and dining hall. It was later converted to staff housing and renamed. When West Camp was completed, a new health lodge was built, which later became the West Camp director's cabin. The current health lodge started as the reservation director's residence.

The East Camp dining hall is seen here in the 1940s. It was one of the most famous buildings erected in the spring of 1929 by the North Shore Area Council, BSA. It was large enough for campers, adult leaders, and staff to eat their meals. It still serves as a dining hall and houses many artifacts from the history of Camp Ma-Ka-Ja-Wan. (Courtesy of Ruby Dalton.)

Shown here is mealtime at the East Camp dining hall in the late 1940s. The dining hall was also used as a center for daily programs featuring songs, skits, and stunts. The dining hall has had many additions, including a porch on the west side and a loading dock on the east side for receiving deliveries. (Courtesy of Ruby Dalton.)

Members of the East Camp dining hall staff are, from left to right, John Sheridan (1955 lodge chief), Stu Malsch, Larry Reuter (1958 lodge chief), Theora Bazille, Arvilla Thorn, and Bill Williams. Both the East and West Camp kitchens are run by a trained and dedicated cook staff. Each camp cook had a specialty, such as baked goods or main courses. Bazille and Thorn served as cooks for many years.

To call Scouts, leaders, and staff members to meals, as well as to alert the camp to emergencies, a staff member would play a bugle call into a megaphone near the dining hall. In later years, this was replaced by a recording over a loudspeaker that could be heard throughout camp.

The first East Camp office (shown here) was built in the spring of 1929. It was the focal point of camp business. This structure now serves as staff housing under the name Hilltop. The first camp director was Carl McManus. He was also assistant scout executive and the first lodge chief for Ma-Ka-Ja-Wan Lodge No. 40.

Each camp has a Shooting Sports area with rifle, shotgun, and archery ranges. The areas are run by a director and support staff trained in BSA safety procedures. The first East Camp Shooting Sports area was located near the old scoutmaster's parking lot, just up the hill from the present East Camp office. It was moved to the outer parts of East Camp in the early 1970s. (Courtesy of Ruby Dalton.)

The original shotgun range in East Camp was of primitive design, but it gave many Boy Scouts their first opportunity to shoot shotguns. Many of the young men attending Camp Ma-Ka-Ja-Wan come from urban or suburban areas. The camp provides exposure to new activities, like skeet-shooting.

In the early years, the chapel was located near the main part of East Camp. It is now located near the south end of Spring Lake. It gives all participants the opportunity to practice their faith. (Courtesy of Hank Jostock.)

The Aquatics area is one of the most popular in camp. Note the original dock and boathouse in this 1948 photograph of East Aquatics. Spring Lake serves as a great center of aquatic activity. The water level is maintained by limiting the flow of water to Skids Creek, near the Whitney campsite. (Courtesy of Ruby Dalton.)

East Aquatics is seen here sometime between 1947 and 1949. Spring Lake is large enough to accommodate different sizes of sailboats. On a good day, enough wind can keep boats sailing all day. One of the larger, faster boats to sail Spring Lake was known as the *Killiani*. (Courtesy of Dick Behan.)

The Dustbowl was used for flag ceremonies and Order of the Arrow Tap Outs since the opening of camp. It also served as a meeting place for campwide games and other activities. In the last two decades, the parade ground was moved to the west side of the East Camp dining hall. The Order of the Arrow Tap Outs moved to the current bowl in the 1950s. (Courtesy of Hank Jostock.)

In 1937, the North Shore Area Council used this photograph as part of its camp promotion brochure, "The Way to Camp Ma-Ka-Ja-Wan." An original of this photograph was presented to Dr. James E. West, the first chief scout executive for the BSA, on May 10, 1937.

Father Leo Belanger and Miss La Chein, staff members in the late 1940s, pose outside the East Camp dining hall. Camp staff in 1947 was mostly adult, with only a handful of youth. David King, one of the youth members that year, remembers it as one of the greatest times of his life.

This is one of the only photographs of the cook staff from the early years. Shown are, from left to right, Laura Skidmore, Ruby Dalton, Arvilla Thorn, Mary Schuk, and Theora Bazille. Each woman gave years to the camp, traveling daily on the barge to work at East Camp. Several have had children and grandchildren on staff and great-grandchildren as campers. The spirit of Ma-Ka-Ja-Wan is clearly part of their legacy. (Courtesy of Ian Hopkins.)

Harold Thorn (left) was an Ainsworth Township resident who served as the camp ranger for three decades. He lived at the camp with his wife, Arvilla. His daughter, Lillyetta, grew up at camp, attended school in Pearson, and met her husband, Larry Trezise, at Camp Ma-Ka-Ja-Wan. They were married at the camp chapel in the 1960s. (Courtesy of the Thorn family.)

Harry Skidmore (right) attended Ma-Ka-Ja-Wan for the first time in the summer of 1929. It was his first trip out of Highland Park, Illinois. He remembers a long train ride, followed by a rough ride in the back of a stake truck to camp from Elcho, Wisconsin. He remained in the Scouting program his entire life, serving as scoutmaster for Troop 324 in Highland Park. He is seen here with Bob Black. (Courtesy of Ian Hopkins.)

Over the years, Ma-Ka-Ja-Wan was enlarged and the numbers of campers increased. It has seen expanded use in the off-season for winter camping, snowshoeing, and cross-country skiing. The name Camp Ma-Ka-Ja-Wan was changed to Ma-Ka-Ja-Wan Scout Reservation in the early 1970s. It was expanded from the original 240 acres to over 1,500 acres.

When Scouts, adult leaders, and visitors arrived at Camp Ma-Ka-Ja-Wan, one of their first sights was this totem pole. It was hand-carved and painted with vibrant colors. It has been moved to near the Country Store in Family Camp.

ADVENTURELAND lies to the North. Less than 300 miles from the Northshore towns lies the land of romance and adventure for the nearly-a-thousand Scouts of the Northshore. The New Camp Site of 360 acres of timber-land and water is located 20 miles northeast of Antigo, Wisconsin, and 14 miles southeast of the little lumbering center of Elcho.

"TALL TIMBER" was one of the names suggested in the vote for a camp name, for in every direction, there stretches, miles of timber-land, suitable for hikes and exploration trips.

"BLUE WATER" was the name suggested by one of the Scoutmasters the moment he came around the bend of the road and saw Spring Lake stretched out before him with its blue waters sparkling under the noon-day sun. The lake is almost a mile long and has a shoreline of over two miles of good beach and high dry shore.

MA-KA-JA-WAN The Menominee Indian name for Spring Lake was selected in a poll of more than 500 votes, for not many miles distant from the camp is the 210,000 acre home of the Menominee Indian Tribe.

This excerpt from the 1929 camp promotion brochure lists some of the proposed names for Ma-Ka-Ja-Wan. The names were proposed and voted on by a selection committee comprised of the Scout executive and key volunteers.

Scouts pose at the south end of Lake Killian around 1982. The lake was named Mosquito Lake prior to the turn of the century. It was given its current official name, Spring Lake, after the turn of the century. It has come to be unofficially known as Lake Killian, after Victor J. Killian, Properties Committee member in the early 1970s.

The mantle in the East Camp dining hall is seen here in 2010. It displays Paul Bunyan's Axe Handle, carved by a young Scout named George Bersch and a group of friends attending camp in the late 1930s. Bersch served on staff and was the 1939 lodge chief. When he visited the camp just a couple of summers ago, prior to his death, he made a point to see the axe handle. (Courtesy of Matt Horbal.)

Two

Order of the Arrow

Steve Silca and Ian Hopkins

Ma-Ka-Ja-Wan Lodge was chartered on May 1, 1929. It was the 40th lodge in the nation to receive a charter since the founding of the Order of the Arrow in 1915. The lodge was the second of eight chartered that year. Dr. E. Urner Goodman, one of the cofounders of the order, was in Chicago at the time and made the trip to Camp Ma-Ka-Ja-Wan to present the charter and install the first officers. Carl McManus, the first camp director and assistant scout executive, was appointed the first lodge chief.

The lodge initially picked the wolf as its totem, but found that another lodge in the nation was already using the wolf. The whippoorwill was then chosen, because of the many whippoorwills at Camp Ma-Ka-Ja-Wan.

The lodge presented the Vigil Honor for the first time in 1932 to George W. Bersch, John F. Betak, and H.G. Boltz.

At the Christmas Banquet on December 12, 1932, the lodge established the fine tradition of the Example. In 1960, the only addition was to have two Examples, one from East Camp and one from West Camp. An honor roll of all Examples is proudly displayed in the Order of the Arrow Lodge.

In the early 1970s, the North Shore Area Council, BSA, merged with two other councils to form the Northeast Illinois Council, BSA. Ma-Ka-Ja-Wan Lodge No. 40 merged with Wabaningo Lodge No. 248 and Noo-Ti-Mis Oh'Ke Lodge No. 215.

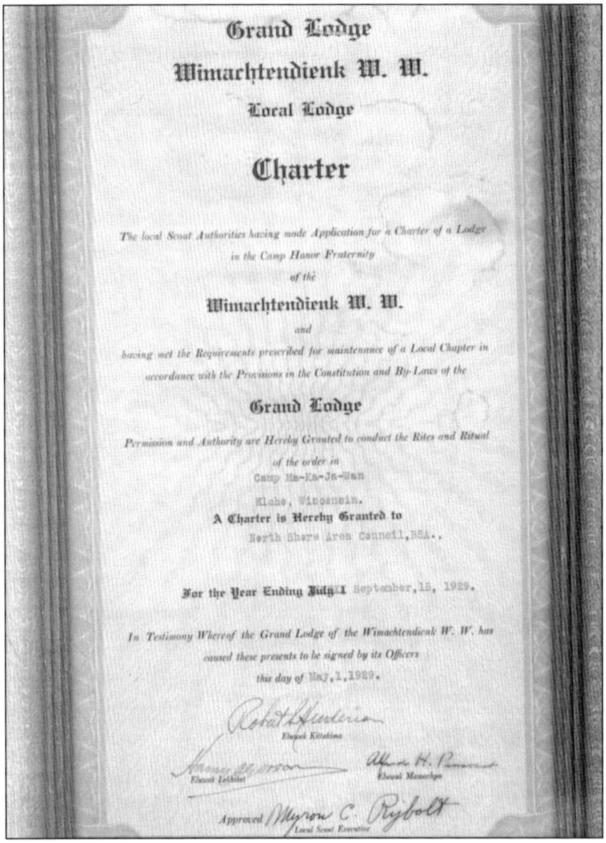

Grand Lodge
Wimachtendienk W. W.
Local Lodge

Charter

The local Scout Authorities having made Application for a Charter of a Lodge in the Camp Honor Fraternity of the

Wimachtendienk W. W.

and having met the Requirements prescribed for maintenance of a Local Chapter in accordance with the Provisions in the Constitution and By-Laws of the

Grand Lodge

Permission and Authority are Hereby Granted to conduct the Rites and Ritual of the order in
Camp Ma-Ka-Ja-Wan
Elcho, Wisconsin.

A Charter is Hereby Granted to
North Shore Area Council, BSA.,

For the Year Ending ~~July 1~~ September, 15, 1929.

In Testimony Whereof the Grand Lodge of the Wimachtendienk W. W. has caused these presents to be signed by its Officers this day of May, 1, 1929.

Robert L. Henderson
Elangomat Kittakima

Eluwak Lekhiket

Alfred H. Pearson
Eluwak Munachpo

Approved Myron C. Rybolt
Local Scout Executive

The grand charter of Ma-Ka-Ja-Wan Lodge No. 40 was presented on May 1, 1929, to the newly installed lodge chief, Carl McManus, by cofounder of the Order of the Arrow, Dr. E Urner Goodman, at Camp Ma-Ka-Ja-Wan.

The fireplace in the Order of the Arrow (OA) Lodge is seen here in 2001, shortly after renovation. The OA Lodge was originally located at the south end of Spring Lake. Initially used as the Siberian Mess Hall by Sea Scouts, it was moved across the lake in 1948. In 1952–1954, a fireplace and windows were installed, and in 1958, the front porch was added. (Courtesy of Matt Horbal.)

Prior to the current Order of the Arrow Bowl, the Callout Ceremony was conducted in the Dustbowl. The staff set up an Indian village at the start of the summer in the Dustbowl and used it for the Indian Lore merit badge. This photograph was taken around 1955. (Courtesy of Hank Jostock.)

The present Order of the Arrow Bowl (shown here) was found in 1957 by camp director Chuck Gribble, hence its other name, "the Grib Bowl." Gribble served on the Camp Ma-Ka-Ja-Wan staff as a camp director and reservation director from 1954 to 1961. He was the first director of West Camp in 1959. (Courtesy of George Christensen.)

Shown here is the OA Bowl third fire, in 2005. From 2003 to 2005, a dedicated crew of volunteers renovated the OA Bowl in the founders' vision. After its renovation, the Grib Bowl was rededicated in memory of Charles J. Gribble. (Courtesy of Kevin Baldwin.)

This is one of the earliest photographs of a Callout Ceremony in the Grib Bowl. Included are the traditional "Hoopies," the original teepee, and the kerosene smudge pots. The fire is lit after an invocation by Meteu, the medicine man.

Each summer, staff members are recruited to be part of the ritual team. They participate in all of the Order of the Arrow ceremonies. The 1957 principals are, from left to right, Dick Siebel, J.D. Brink, Don Verbeke (lodge chief), and Larry Reuter. (Courtesy of George Christensen.)

At the hands of the chief, each candidate is congratulated for being chosen, as is the Scout in this photograph. This begins the testing and service of the Ordeal. After going through a testing period, the Scout is honored at a special induction ceremony. At that time, each new member receives his Ordeal sash. The Ordeal is an experience that Scouts remember for the rest of their lives.

The 1973 Vigil Ritual Team poses for a photograph. They are, from left to right, Michael Tager, Tracy Page, Jim Chandler, and Roger Irland. The Vigil Honor, the highest honor awarded by the Order of the Arrow, is presented to those who show untiring service to the Boy Scouts and to the order. (Courtesy of Lloyd Moon.)

After each Vigil Honor induction, a group photograph is taken to document the event. Shown here is the 1963 Vigil class. Many of these photographs were taken by Lloyd Moon, who became a Vigil Honor member in 1947. (Courtesy of Lloyd Moon.)

In 1976, the lodge was led by Lodge Chief Ken Gordon. He is pictured here with the members of the 1976 Ritual Team. From left to right are (first row) Joe Behles and Ron Chrzanowski; (second row) Gordon, Don Sesterhenn, and Honorsmaster Neil Brock. After serving as honorsmaster, Brock became lodge chief in 1977. (Courtesy of Mike Creagh.)

One of the traditional parts of the Callout Ceremony was the Flaming Hoop Dance. The dancers emerged from pits at the start of the ceremony, which began with a flaming arrow shot by the runner. The Hoop Dance was replaced with the Grass Dance in 1994.

Prior to every Callout Ceremony, there are extensive preparations, including construction of the council fire, the practice and planning of the ceremony, and creation of the handmade regalia. This is a photograph of the 1979 Ritual Team, under the leadership of Lodge Chief Ken Beauvais (second row, far right) and Honorsmaster Mark Gaines (second row, far left). (Courtesy of Bob King.)

Each member puts in hours of preparation for the Callout and Induction Ceremonies. Each year, new members of the team learn the ropes from experienced members. The Order of the Arrow continues as an integral part of the Camp Ma-Ka-Ja-Wan summer program. Pictured here is the 2012 Ritual Team, under the leadership of Lodge Chief Sam Gartzman and Honorsmaster Sean Thoms (not pictured). (Courtesy of Nick Hill.)

Ma-Ka-Ja-Wan Lodge No. 40 of the Order of the Arrow is led by a youth member voted to serve as lodge chief. He is elected by his peers for a one-year term. This is a true honor, and it has weighty responsibilities for a young person. Traditionally, the lodge chief takes the persona of Allowat Sakima in summer ceremonies. Pictured here is Lodge Chief Kevin Beauvais.

Near the beginning of the ceremony, Meteu says a prayer and throws symbolic dust toward the council fire, causing it to magically light. Many staff members have played this role over the years. Pictured here is Tony Mockus of Evanston, Illinois. (Courtesy of Michael Swanson.)

To prepare for the Callout Ceremony, staff and Order of the Arrow members have nightly work projects to construct the fire and prepare the bowl. The process is overseen by a group of staff members known as the OA Rangers. This group also works with the ranger staff to provide fire protection during the ceremony.

After being called out the evening before, new members of the Order of the Arrow spend the day completing their Ordeal by working on service projects around Camp Ma-Ka-Ja-Wan. These projects help make the camp a better place and teach the virtues of cheerful service. (Courtesy of Hank Jostock.)

Ordeal members can seal their membership in the Order of the Arrow by earning the Brotherhood Honor. New Brotherhood members are called out during a flag ceremony. Here, Clark Llamzon (in regalia) calls out a new Brotherhood member, who will spend the next day leading work crews of Ordeal candidates in service projects.

As stated in the "Lodge No. 40 History," "At the Christmas Banquet, December 12, 1932, the Lodge established the fine tradition of the Example. This was to honor a Scout of the Brotherhood [or Vigil] honor who had best exemplified Cheerful Service to take the Ordeal along with the new Candidates." At the conclusion of every Callout Ceremony, Examples are called. Here, Mike Schaeffer Jr. (third from left) and Derek Coleman (second from left) are called during the First Fire in 2005. (Courtesy of Matt Horbal.)

The Camp Ma-Ka-Ja-Wan fire truck, a 1948 Ford F-6, continues to serve and extinguish OA fires, as it has since the 1970s. In 2001, Scouts and adult leaders of Troop 198 from Mundelein, Illinois, repaired and restored the truck to its former glory. The troop undertook the task under the vision and leadership of Scoutmaster David Bruecks. (Courtesy of Matt Horbal.)

This sign at the base of the OA Trail has been passed under by thousands of Scouts on their way to the Callout Ceremony in the OA Bowl. From at least the early 1960s, it has marked the start of the path that leads up a steep grade to the edge of the Order of the Arrow Bowl.

Three

West Camp

Joe Jordan

As the number of Boy Scouts in the North Shore Area Council, BSA, increased, it was imperative to add more acreage to Camp Ma-Ka-Ja-Wan. Under the leadership of Scout Executive Edwin A. Schwechel and a volunteer steering committee, it was decided to purchase more plots of land around Spring Lake. One of those plots was a farm on the west side of the lake. The land was owned by Burnam Skidmore and had an access road to the lakefront. Sometime in the mid-1950s, Skidmore sold the land to the North Shore Area Council, BSA. The access road was used to bring the Boy Scouts and adult leaders to the West Barge Dock, where they loaded their gear. The barge then took their gear across the lake, and the scouts and adult leaders would walk around the north end of the lake to the East Camp office to check in. The design of West Camp was confirmed in the late 1950s, and a road around the south end of the lake was built, making it easier to deliver material and other supplies to East Camp. In the spring of 1959, the main structures in West Camp had been completed and were ready to be occupied. By that time, Camp Ma-Ka-Ja-Wan included East Camp, West Camp, and Family Camp. Each sub-camp opened the doors for more Boy Scouts, adult leaders, and families to attend summer camp. The camp began to be used in the fall, winter, and spring.

Under the direction of North Shore Area Scout Executive Edwin A. Schwechel (shown here), plans were developed for West Camp and the road to East Camp. A camp expansion campaign was conducted in 1957, an outcome of the development of the council's long-range plan, which produced funds making the construction of West Camp possible.

Charles Lauzon (1920–2009) was the architect who designed many of the buildings in West Camp. The original plan included a dining hall, camp office, handicraft lodge, nature lodge, and trading post/quartermaster building, as well as a boathouse on the west side of Lake Killian.

After the building of West Camp, a program was created to plant a pine tree grove to the north of the present West Camp Field. That grove, host to the first West Camp Firebowl, presently shades the West Trailblazer area. Planting the trees in 1956 are, from left to right, Jim Butterworth, George Christensen, Don Verbeke, and Bob Brehends. (Courtesy of Don Verbeke.)

The West Camp office is shown here under construction in June 1959. Note the absence of pine trees and the road headed directly across the West Camp Field. This office still serves as the command post of West Camp.

The inaugural West Camp staff is pictured on August 13, 1959, outside the West Camp dining hall. Among those shown here are Chuck Gribble (second row, sixth from left), Jon Haring (second row, far right), Arvilla Thorn (second row, seventh from left), and Mike Birdlebough (first row, third from right). Many of these individuals remained involved in Ma-Ka-Ja-Wan for their entire lives.

This is an early aerial view of West Camp in the off season. The West Camp waterfront is in the foreground. The pine forest was planted in 1956. The notch halfway up the right side of the "L" is the old West Camp Firebowl. Note that the road used to run diagonally from the dining hall, across the field, to the waterfront.

The West Camp trading post and quartermaster building is seen here under construction in the late 1950s. Note the absence of the pine trees that today surround and tower over the building. Also missing is the climbing wall area to the north of the trading post and quartermaster building.

Clark Llamzon is pictured inside the newly renovated West Camp trading post and quartermaster building. The trading post occupies the left half of the building, and the quartermaster the right half. Both had windows that opened into the center section. During renovation in 2004, the breezeway was enclosed and the trading post was expanded by the Wilderness Engineering Society (WES). (Courtesy of Steve Silca.)

An adult leader checks out an Indian pump from the West Camp quartermaster. This was high-tech firefighting equipment for Ma-Ka-Ja-Wan at the time. Some of the equipment is still in use over 50 years later.

The obstacle course was built in the West Camp Field, just north of the Handicraft Lodge. It was designed to provide an opportunity for the Scouts at summer camp to work on physical fitness and to have friendly patrol and troop competitions. In its heyday, the obstacle course had climbing walls, rope swings, a balance beam, and tires to maneuver through, among other features. It also served as a great location for the 1972 West Camp staff photograph.

This 1960 photograph shows the original West Camp Scoutcraft/Handicraft Lodge. The two areas shared halves of the same building. The Handicraft Lodge is pictured above. Decades later, Scoutcraft would be moved to a location in the middle of the pine forest. It has moved several times since then and spun off the Trailblazer area.

Here, campers and leaders eat in the West Camp dining hall. The flags surrounding the fireplace are from the 1960 National Boy Scout Jamboree in Colorado Springs. The banner on the left is from the Philmont Trek in 1963.

The West Camp dining hall is pictured shortly after construction. Note the vintage car and the absence of later additions to accommodate increasing food storage and preparation requirements. The Wilderness Engineering Society recently added a propane-powered backup generator to keep the freezers running during power outages.

This is the West Camp dining hall as it looks today. It and all other camp buildings used to be painted beige, but they were painted dark brown in the early 1970s. It was often joked that the "price was right" on the brown paint. On the left is one of the many additions to the back of the dining hall. (Courtesy of Matt Horbal.)

Located just outside the dining hall, the West Camp flagpole is one of the most picturesque sights in camp. When camp is in session, each day begins and ends with a flag ceremony attended by the West Camp staff and all the campers and leaders in West Camp. (Courtesy of Matt Ludmer.)

Located north of the trading post, the climbing wall area is a relatively new addition to West Camp. Serving both camps, the climbing wall was built in the late 1990s and offers instruction for the Climbing merit badge and Climb on Safely training. (Courtesy of Matt Horbal.)

The West Camp waterfront is seen here in its early years. Note the much smaller boathouse and the twin rafts, all of which have since been replaced. Still in service is the lookout chair, seen here just in front of the boathouse window. Today, this is the Aquatics facility. The lake is still as clean and refreshing as it has always been.

Construction is in progress on the "new" West Camp Aquatics boathouse in the spring of 1995. The project is one of many completed by the Wilderness Engineering Society. This boathouse continues to serve the campers and staff of West Camp Aquatics. (Courtesy of Ambrose Cantagallo.)

The West Camp Ecology-Conservation (Eco-Con) Lodge is seen here in 2003. This building was renovated and expanded by members of the Wilderness Engineering Society in the early 2010s. It was referred to as the Nature Lodge prior to the 1980s. (Courtesy of Matt Horbal.)

Seen here in 2003 is the rifle range at West Camp Shooting Sports. The area teaches rifle, shotgun, and archery shooting as well as safety and maintenance. It is located between the Cody and Crockett campsites. (Courtesy of Kevin Baldwin.)

This is a view of Lake Killian from the West Camp Firebowl. The Firebowl was originally located in the pine forest between the present-day Trailblazer area and the campers' shower house. It was moved to its present location on the shores of Lake Killian in 1989. (Courtesy of Kevin Baldwin.)

Affectionately named the Bungalows, these structures on West Staff Row provide housing to junior staff. Pictured here in the early 1990s, the bungalows were moved into a straight line along the road in the mid-1990s to facilitate an upgrade to underground electrical service. They enjoy a delightful view of Lake Killian and a central West Camp location.

Four

FAMILY CAMP

Family Camp, located along the west shore of Lake Killian, south of West Camp, began in the early 1950s. The land that is now Family Camp originally was a resort dating to the turn of the 20th century. It became a facility for the families of Scout leaders who came to Camp Ma-Ka-Ja-Wan for summer vacations. To attract more families, the North Shore Area Council added additional cabins, a swimming area, playground, dining hall, and other facilities. Some of the cabins that are currently in use were part of the resort, while others were later additions. The Family Camp dining hall was converted to the Country Store in the early 1970s and now serves as a general store. Over the past 20 years, the Family Camp cabins have been renovated and updated, due to the efforts of the Wilderness Engineering Society. While fewer families travel to Ma-Ka-Ja-Wan these days, the cabins are now used more frequently to house camp staff and volunteers.

The first swimming area at Family Camp was cleared by the Schwechel and Thorn families. They spent hours clearing seaweed from the area and placing sand in the swimming area to make it better for the families to use. They provided a qualified lifeguard and instructional swims. Presently, the Family Camp waterfront is used as a launch for fishing boats.

The Country Store (right) was built originally as a dining hall for the families who attended Camp Ma-Ka-Ja-Wan's Family Camp. As with meals served to the Boy Scouts and adult leaders in the camp dining halls, meals were served family style. During the early 1970s, the Family Camp dining hall was converted to what is now called the Country Store.

Some of the newest Family Camp cabins were built north of the main part of Family Camp. These cabins are presently numbered one through five. They were equipped with a small kitchen, a bathroom, and two or three bedrooms. Each cabin has running water, a wood-burning stove for heat, a cooking stove, and a refrigerator.

A Scout leader's spouse and daughter prepare coffee in a Family Camp cabin kitchen. The kitchen was basic, but it was used throughout their stay at Camp Ma-Ka-Ja-Wan. In the early years, most families would eat in the Family Camp dining hall.

During the day, families would socialize with each other, as seen here outside present-day Cabin 7. There were opportunities to do crafts, take hikes, and visit the other camps. Most of the families came from different towns, but by the end of their stay at Camp Ma-Ka-Ja-Wan, they had made lifelong friends.

On a beautiful summer day, Family Camp guests enjoy a cup of coffee and time relaxing with friends. In the background are the present-day Cabin 14 on the hill and the Country Store on the right.

Five

Camp Wabaningo

Robert G. King, Ranger/Administrator 1967–1984

Late in the 1960s, Camp Ma-Ka-Ja-Wan was beginning to expand. With the merger of the Evanston Boy Scout Council and the closing of its camp in Michigan, it became necessary to look for additional property to allow Ma-Ka-Ja-Wan to handle the increase in the number of Scouts within the new council.

The most logical acquisition was the adjoining property, the Rabe farm. This property, consisting of farm fields and pastureland, comprised about 200 acres, general farm buildings, a two-story house, and a large barn. The farm, owned and operated by Harry and Tede Rabe, was a dairy farm. At the time, Harry Rabe was in ill health, and it was necessary for him to dispose of the property. Another 80 acres, adjoining the Rabe Farm and camp property, were acquired from G.A. Sambs and Theo Prince.

In April 1969, the council purchased land that expanded the camp property borders to County Highway T. This fronted the highway for approximately one fourth of a mile, except for the Ainsworth Township Cemetery.

Following the purchase of the land, the Rabe family continued to operate the farm until the death of Harry Rabe. His wife and mother then vacated the house, which the council then rented for several years into the early 1970s.

In 1970, under the leadership of Scout Executive Alwyn Hughes, the North Shore–Evanston Area Council actively pursued the acquisition of adjoining land located west of Highway T. This was the Luderas property, formerly owned by E.J. Hopfensperger. This parcel comprised nearly 700 acres of forested land, a 30-acre lake, farm buildings and field, and an active body of water, Pickerel Creek. Old logging roads offered access to all areas of the property. A logging railroad bed cut through the property, traversing from south to northeast. It is now the road leading to Triangle M Ranch from the barn.

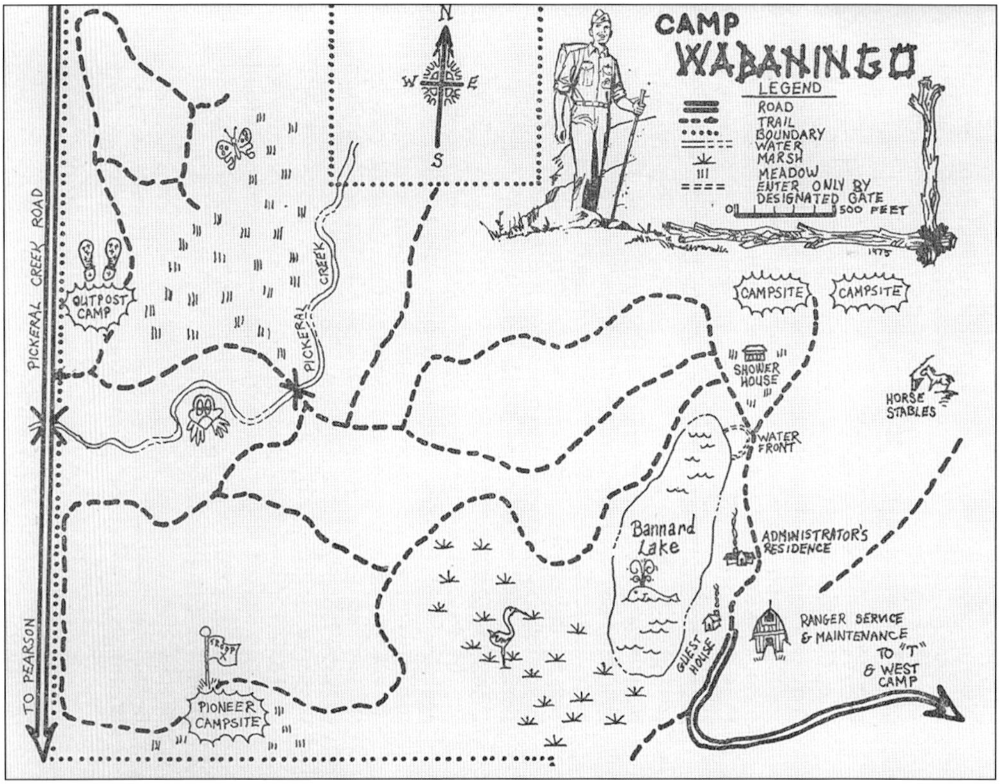

The land was originally developed as an operating dairy farm and a Northwoods lodge. The original owner, E.J. Hopfensperger, was called "the Sausage King of Sheboygan." He had his home and a guest cottage constructed of full logs from trees on the property. The dairy farm was operated by a local caretaker, who ran the farm and lived in the guesthouse. The property was sold to Gilbert Luderas Jr. in the early 1960s, and the dairy operation was discontinued. (Courtesy of Bob King.)

The barn was a traditional Wisconsin-style structure large enough to handle nearly 40 dairy cattle with supporting areas such as feed rooms, machinery storage, repair shops, and second-story hayloft. The outbuildings included a machine storage shed, small animal shelter, silo, and milk storage room, plus other miscellaneous buildings supporting the farm operation. Here, members of the Wilderness Engineering Society work on tent platform construction in 1980. (Courtesy of Ambrose Cantagallo.)

On December 30, 1970, the North Shore–Evanston Council, BSA, entered a contract with Gilbert Luderas Jr. to purchase the property, comprising approximately 620 acres. The addition of the Luderas property brought the total size of the camp to nearly 1,600 acres. In recognition of the old Evanston Boy Scout Council, the new property was named Camp Wabaningo, after the camp in Michigan that was closed soon after the merger.

The barn was probably the most valuable acquisition for camp operations. All maintenance and storage had been housed in the metal Butler Building, located near the camp entrance. Beginning in 1971, the barn was remodeled, as it was largely as it had been at the discontinuation of the dairy operation. Larry Newman, a former camp ranger, is pictured at center with other members of the maintenance staff.

Following the removal of dairy equipment, plans were formed to section off portions of the barn into several departments. The area where the cow stanchions were located became a long workbench. There were two vehicle bays in the north end. The old wooden doors were replaced with overhead doors, and the old milk house was converted into a restroom. (Courtesy of Hank Jostock.)

In the spring of 1972, members of the Wilderness Engineering Society constructed a stairway from the main barn to the loft and built storage cubicles on either side of the loft and open storage on top of the cubicles. At the north end of the loft an area was left open, and a basketball hoop was installed for staff members. (Courtesy of Hank Jostock.)

Access to the loft was provided by the construction of a ramp to loading-dock height for trucks. In addition, an overhead door was installed. The ramp was constructed by John Stewart, a local bricklayer and concrete contractor. (Courtesy of Hank Jostock.)

Adorning the south end of the barn and visible as a visitor rounds the last turn into the maintenance complex is a large fleur-de-lis logo painted on the barn by David Smith. His work also decorates several of the reservation staff paddles that hang in the administration building. (Courtesy of Jim Chandler.)

Following the signing of the land contract in December 1970, one of the first activities was the addition of horses for trail rides and for the Horsemanship merit badge. For the summer of 1974, horses were leased from a local farm and a wrangler was hired for the staff. The wrangler and his assistant, along with volunteers, helped construct horse corrals and fencing, creating the Triangle M Ranch.

Along with the addition of horses to the program, the acquisition of several head of beef cattle to the program gave ranch participants the experience of being a true ranch hand. The farm operation was developed, and a hay crop was harvested each year for livestock feeding. The cattle and farm program were discontinued after several years of operation. (Courtesy of Steve King.)

During the second year of operation of Wabaningo, areas were designated as "outpost camping" for stays by groups coming from East and West Camps on overnight expeditions. An area southwest of the central camp became Pioneer Campsite (shown here). A latrine/washstand was constructed, and a well point was driven with a hand pump.

To address long-term camping needs, a shower was later constructed at the north end of a large field, named Gilwell Field in recognition of the first Woodbadge course conducted at Gilwell in England. This area was used in the 1970s for Woodbadge courses and today hosts annual National Youth Leadership Training sessions. (Courtesy of Jim Chandler.)

Ma-Ka-Ja-Wan Winter Fun

EXPERIENCE Ma-Ka-Ja-Wan in a completely different and exciting way . . . exchange your hiking boots and canoe paddle for skis, snowshoes and toboggan. See the Northwoods in all its winter glory at Ma-Ka-Ja-Wan Winter Adventure Base.

Weekend adventures begin the first week in January and continue through the middle of March. A typical weekend will begin on Friday evening and continue through Sunday noon.

The *Farm House* is the headquarters for all winter activities. This facility can provide accommodations for 35. There are two dormitories with bunks and mattresses, as well as two bedrooms for leaders. Meals are prepared and served by experienced cooks in the upstairs dining room. Central heating, hot showers and modern toilet facilities are all provided.

Over 20 miles of marked cross-country ski trails are maintained on camp property, as well as an exciting toboggan run. Advanced skiers and beginners alike will find the trails a challenge to their individual skills.

Scouts and Leaders of Troop 150, Deerfield, Illinois

The article shown here is from the 1981 issue of *Smoke Signals*, the promotional newsletter for Ma-Ka-Ja-Wan. Although short-lived, the Farm House winter experience was very popular with the troops, who would spend winter weekends in the farmhouse. (Courtesy of Bob King.)

The guest cabin (shown here) and lake in Wabaningo, officially known as Hindu Lake, were named in honor of longtime volunteer and contributor to the North Shore and Northeast Illinois Council, Hibbard Bannard. Today, Bannard Cabin serves as year-round guest quarters for visitors to Ma-Ka-Ja-Wan.

Six

High Adventure

Paul Jordan and John Lillstrom

Prior to 1974, trips taken off the Ma-Ka-Ja-Wan Scout Reservation were primarily overnight canoe trips on the Wolf River, near the camp. Jamie Olson was on staff as the Voyager in the early 1970s, and he would have Scouts hike out of camp to where the canoe trip began. They would hike back to camp at the end of the canoe trip carrying all of their gear, food, and clothes on their back. The High Adventure program at Ma-Ka-Ja-Wan started in 1974, which was the first year that Robert G. King served as the Ma-Ka-Ja-Wan administrator. King had previously served as the camp ranger for many years and was beginning to make changes to the program.

Since the conception of the High Adventure program, it has provided an opportunity for young people and adult leaders to participate in many programs, including rafting, canoe trips, horseback riding, and backpacking treks. Each program was designed to provide additional opportunities for more experienced campers.

In later years, many more programs were added to the High Adventure arsenal to draw more young people to Ma-Ka-Ja-Wan. Recent additions include trips to the Flambeau Flowage, Boundary Waters, and the Apostle Islands.

Bob King, ranger and administrator from 1968 to 1984, stands on the porch of the gatehouse with the 1979 national accreditation placard. The gatehouse served as the administration building prior to the current building of the same name across the street. Today, the gatehouse serves as staff housing. (Courtesy of Steve King.)

In 1974, Paul Jordan (right) was hired to serve as the first High Adventure program director. He had been on the camp staff since 1971, when he served as an assistant provisional scoutmaster under Bob Brown and worked in Scoutcraft the next two years. He was instrumental in carrying out Bob King's vision. (Courtesy of the Thorn family.)

In general, the High Adventure program consisted of off-reservation excursions and canoe trips and involved setting up new experiences for Scouts. Allen Wallentowski, owner of a nearby ranch with trail horses, was contacted to bring Scouts to his ranch for trail rides. Rubber rafts had been purchased or donated from the North Shore, with the plan of finding a spot on the Wolf River where Scouts could raft.

As the opening of camp drew near and regular staff started arriving, details of the High Adventure program had not really been discussed. A team went to A-Bridge to see what was downstream. Paul Jordan and David Weeks (a nature area staff member) boarded a raft at the A-Bridge and headed downstream. That trip did not last long, and the water had no rapids. (Courtesy of John Lillstrom.)

A better location was found about 40 miles south, where the Wolf River crosses through the Gardner Dam Scout Camp. At this location, strong Class III rapids existed. In 1979, the raft team program was run by raft trip team members Sherman Garner (left) and A.J. Roddenbush (right). To deliver the participants and rafts to and from the trip, the bus was outfitted with a large roof rack. (Courtesy of Bob King.)

Kim Goluska (not pictured) was High Adventure program director in 1976. He started on staff in 1974 as the East Camp dining lodge director. In 1975, while on the ranger staff, he started pilot trips to the Porcupine Mountains State Park along Lake Superior. The Porkies Trip is a backpacking hike of four to five days, outfitted by Ma-Ka-Ja-Wan. The expedition is offered to this day.

By 1976, a stable was built on the Wabaningo side of camp to house horses on camp property. Bob Farris ran the ranch, and Goluska would use the bus for rubber-raft trips and Porkies Trips. Mike Carew helped run the rubber raft trips as well. In 1976, along with trail rides, overnight chuck wagon trips were begun. On these excursions, Scouts on horseback would have a trail dinner and campfire. (Courtesy of Bob King.)

John Lillstrom (shown here) took over as High Adventure program director in 1977. He started on staff in 1975 and 1976 as West Camp nature director. During Lillstrom's tenure, the rubber-raft trips continued, as did the Porkies trips and the ranch. John Kyle, another longtime staff member, assisted with the Porkies trips and raft trips. (Courtesy of John Lillstrom.)

Ranch Foreman Ed Hoolehan (right) and Wrangler Scott Nelson (left) sit on the front porch of the Triangle M Ranch bunkhouse. Hoolehan, one of the first foremen of the ranch, was instrumental in developing the Ranch program. He ran the ranch from 1976 to 1979. (Courtesy of Bob King.)

The Ranch program continues to be one of the most popular at Ma-Ka-Ja-Wan. On a daily basis, ranch staff lead Scouts and adults on trail rides around Camp Wabaningo. Scouts are seen here riding through the horse pasture. They also teach Horsemanship and Animal Science merit badges.

The 2012 High Adventure staff earned the National Inspection "A" rating from the Boy Scouts of America for their superb efforts in the program and the high level of running treks out of the Camp Ma-Ka-Ja-Wan High Adventure base. The staff worked under the direction of John Lillstrom, High Adventure coordinator (first row, left), and Rurik Fencl, High Adventure director (first row, right). (Courtesy of John Lillstrom.)

In 2011, backpacking trips were taken to Pictured Rock National Lakeshore, and kayak trips were conducted at the Apostle Islands in Bayfield, Wisconsin. John Lillstrom, the High Adventure program coordinator in 2012, added canoe trips on the Flambeau River and in the Sylvania Wilderness. This photograph is from a 2013 Flambeau trek.

From the rodeos of the Triangle M Ranch of the 1970s to the expanded offering of treks today, not to mention Buckskin and the Black Hole, the High Adventure program continues to offer new and exciting activities to Scouts. New generations of staff members have risen to the task of taking the program to the next level. (Courtesy of Steve King.)

The basic idea of the High Adventure program was to expand experiences for Scouts. What began with an exploratory trip down the Wolf River, with the vision of Robert G. King, and the hard work and passion provided by Paul Jordan, Kim Goluska, John Lillstrom, Ed Hoolehan, and many others, became a program serving the Scouts of Ma-Ka-Ja-Wan for nearly four decades.

Seven

Wilderness Engineering Society

Jim Chandler and Ian Hopkins

The very first Workers' Weekend at Ma-Ka-Ja-Wan can be traced to 1928, even before it was a formal Scout camp. That summer, Ambrose Cantagallo and a few other young men were recruited to clear spots and prepare other physical needs in readiness for the opening in 1929.

It is unknown when the official label of Workers' Weekend was applied to the annual volunteer maintenance efforts at Ma-Ka-Ja-Wan. It is known, however, that the term was used at least in the early 1950s, when weekends were led by Victor J. Killian.

Jim Chandler's first encounter with the Workers' Weekend was in 1964, when the Camping Committee was chaired by Alan G. Moore and the Properties Committee was chaired by Vic Killian. The weekend, held each spring in May, was titled Workers' Weekend through 1971. Jim Chandler, as the council director of program, was responsible for advising the Properties Committee, at which time he suggested that the name Wilderness Engineering Society be applied to the informal group of skilled and unskilled volunteers who participated in Workers' Weekends. Thus, the Wilderness Engineering Society was born in the spring of 1972. That same year, the Workers' Weekend was expanded into two weekends, one in the spring and one in the fall.

In 1973, Delroy Haggie replaced Ambrose as the leader of the Wilderness Engineering Society. He also was appointed chairman of the Camping Committee. Haggie was instrumental in increasing the number and types of skilled tradesmen who volunteered time and effort to these maintenance/construction weekends.

After Haggie retired as chief engineer, Sylvester Reitmeyer and Don "Swanie" Swanson served in that position for a year. Following Swanson's tenure, John Hopkins was appointed chief engineer. He serves in that position to this day.

The Wilderness Engineering Society has continued to be the prime factor in providing untold and immeasurable gifts of in-kind labor and material, which keep Ma-Ka-Ja-Wan facilities in their admirable physical condition.

Victor J. Killian, seen here second from left in Family Camp, served as properties chair from the North Shore Area Council. He was very instrumental in the development of Workers' Weekends, beginning in the early 1950s to support Camp Ma-Ka-Ja-Wan. In recognition of his efforts and contributions, Spring Lake was unofficially renamed "Lake Killian." (Courtesy of Lloyd Moon.)

Ambrose Cantagallo was a force at Ma-Ka-Ja-Wan over his 80-year tenure in Scouting. He became a Scout in Troop 31 from Highwood, Illinois, in 1926. He joined the camp staff in 1931 as a health lodge assistant. Cantagallo served in many unit positions and at the council level on the Properties Committee and Executive Board. He was part of the original group that grew to become the WES. (Courtesy of Jim Chandler.)

Delroy Haggie (left) took over leadership of the Wilderness Engineering Society from Ambrose Cantagallo. He also served as the chairman of the Properties Committee for the North Shore Area Council. Haggie is seen here with Woody Coughenour. (Courtesy of Jim Chandler.)

Don Tiffany served as the WES chairman and as chairman of the Council Camping Committee, overseeing the physical properties and program at Ma-Ka-Ja-Wan. Working with many volunteers, Don created the template, still in use today, on how the Properties Committee runs and why it must consider the program and its impact on the buildings and grounds before repairs, alterations, or new builds are conducted. (Courtesy of Irene Tiffany.)

Al Moore (left) and Bob King eat in the West Camp dining hall during a Workers' Weekend. Moore was very active in the Wilderness Engineering Society, organizing work projects, securing materials, and acquiring funding for projects. (Courtesy of Jim Chandler.)

Jim Chandler, program director for the Northshore Area Council, BSA, is giving direction to Wilderness Engineering Society members during a meal. Every mealtime, the plans for the day's projects are discussed and adjustments are made so the projects can be completed. It is also a time to recognize members of the Wilderness Engineering Society for their exceptional service and contributions. (Courtesy of Jim Chandler).

A work crew during a Workers' Weekend pour a cement slab. Members of the WES have worked and built many of the buildings at Ma-Ka-Ja-Wan. Chuck Gravitter is at far left, and Peter Cooper is third from left. (Courtesy of Jim Chandler.)

When the new health lodge was built, it became a facility that served East and West campers, High Adventure participants, and camp staff. It was staffed by volunteer nurses, Navy corpsmen, and EMTs. The concrete stairs that lead up to the health lodge were installed by members of the Wilderness Engineering Society during their many work weekends. The health lodge continues to be in use today. (Courtesy of Jim Chandler.)

Brian McIlwee works on the Gillwell Field shower house. This building, still in use today, provides facilities for the Scouts and adult leaders who do wilderness camping at Camp Wabaningo and who participate during Wood Badge and Brownsea training courses. (Courtesy of Jim Chandler.)

The Wilderness Engineering Society has been working on the remodeling of the Country Store for many years. In this photograph, a WES member works on rehabbing the Country Store in the early 1970s. In 2010 and 2011, the WES started interior work of the Country Store. Nels and Gina Rohzon were the team, with Tom Moore and other volunteers, who installed counters and shelving. (Courtesy of Jim Chandler.)

The Wilderness Engineering Society built the new East Camp Shooting Sports shelter in the early 1970s. The original location was near the old scoutmaster's parking lot, near the East Camp office. Starting in 2011, the East Shooting Sports area was reconfigured and updated. (Courtesy of Jim Chandler.)

Wilderness Engineering Society members do electrical work on a building that would later become the OA shed, used for storage of equipment and sand paint at the Order of the Arrow Bowl. It was demolished by the WES in the fall of 2009. Prior to its use at the OA Bowl, it was used as the outpost commissary, located near the present-day scoutmaster's parking lot. (Courtesy of Jim Chandler.)

During work weekends at Camp Ma-Ka-Ja-Wan, a cook staff is enlisted to prepare and serve meals for attendees. The cook staff members pictured here are John Hays (left) and Woody Coughenour. On every weekend, between 50 and 70 individuals attend the work sessions. To thank the workers for coming to camp, the council provides meals at no cost. (Courtesy of Jim Chandler.)

At Workers' Weekends, a volunteer delivers snacks and drinks to the laborers. In this case, it is Scoutmaster George Ergang (in plaid shirt) who has volunteered for the task. The vehicle has been affectionately named the "coffeewagon." (Courtesy of Jim Chandler.)

After a long day working on projects at Camp Ma-Ka-Ja-Wan, three members of the Wilderness Engineering Society have coffee in front of the fireplace in the West Camp dining hall. In the spring, the mornings and evenings are often cool, and the fireplace provides a source of warmth during meals. Woody Coughenour is at center, and Gene Nero is at right. (Courtesy of Jim Chandler.)

A crew works in the lower part of the newly renovated maintenance barn. The workbench and radial-arm saw (shown here) were installed where the cow stanchions were located at the time the property was acquired. The maintenance barn is still in use today. (Courtesy of Jim Chandler.)

Several crew members work on renovating the upper barn, the area formerly used as a hayloft. The Wilderness Engineering Society constructed a loft and storage cubicles that now serve as a storehouse of spare equipment. The members of the WES and Properties Committee put a plan in place to maintain the facilities at Ma-Ka-Ja-Wan. (Courtesy of Jim Chandler.)

Bill Runnion is pictured painting one of the four-man tents on West Staff Row. The four-man tents were later removed, but the two-man versions were converted to the bungalows that are still in use today. This is one example of how numerous members of the construction trades, former and present staff members, as well as other volunteers continue to improve and maintain Camp Ma-Ka-Ja-Wan. (Courtesy of Jim Chandler.)

Eight

The Remembrance Area

Ian Hopkins

The Remembrance Area at Camp Ma-Ka-Ja-Wan was the vision of several past staff members. The project came to life when members of Ma-Ka-Ja-Wan Lodge No. 40 of the Order of the Arrow and the Wilderness Engineering Society joined forces.

The purpose of the Remembrance Area is to honor those young people, adult leaders, and members of organizations attached to the camp who have passed away.

The location of the Remembrance Area was picked due to its proximity to the camp chapel. The relationship between the Remembrance Area and the chapel emphasizes the 12th point of the Scout Law: A Scout is Reverent.

The Remembrance Area was built in the spring of 2001 under the leadership of Michael Landgraf and members of the Order of the Arrow. The project was funded in part by a grant from the National Order of the Arrow Office in Irving, Texas. Prior to construction, the materials were purchased and the area was cleared. During construction, Landgraf and his team built three display stands. They also built an entryway to the area.

In the spring of 2004, the area was completed with the installation of three display boards. The display boards will hold the names of up to 396 honorees.

The Remembrance Area was dedicated on July 4, 2004. Over 100 Scouts, adult leaders, staff members, and family members of the first class of Remembrance Area honorees were in attendance. During the dedication, a special chapel service was conducted. The attendees heard the new Ma-Ka-Ja-Wan prayer, written by Steve Silca, a former staff member.

Since its dedication, the Remembrance Area has become an integral part of the program at Camp Ma-Ka-Ja-Wan. The area has become a place of honor where guests can stop and reflect. Many family members come back to the Remembrance Area to view the names of their loved ones. (Courtesy of Steve Silca.)

From left to right, Order of the Arrow members Mike Landgraf, unidentified, Brady Mark, and Greg Gilpin build the Remembrance Area at Camp Ma-Ka-Ja-Wan. The work crew was led by architect Michael Landgraf, who designed the area. The area includes three display boards, representing the three parts of the Scout Oath. In later years, a triangular seating area was added in the center for visitors. (Courtesy of Matt Horbal.)

Prior to the dedication of the Remembrance Area, Steve Silca designed and built the plaques that would be used to display the honorees' names. He built and stained the plaques and had a local company make the corner and heading plates. The corner plaques would include the symbols for the Wilderness Engineering Society, the Order of the Arrow, the Northeast Illinois Council, and the Ma-Ka-Ja-Wan Scout Reservation. (Courtesy of Steve Silca.)

In the spring of 2004, Steve Silca (front) and Ian Hopkins install the plaques and tempered glass to the three display stands in the Remembrance Area. Each plaque will hold up to 120 names of honorees. Candidates for inclusion are suggested by friends or family members. Following a vetting process, names are engraved on a plate and included in the area. (Courtesy of Steve Silca.)

The Remembrance Area was dedicated on July 4, 2004, with over 100 guests in attendance. During the ceremony, several speakers gave testimonials, and the camp staff led the group in song as well as in a responsive reading on the 12 points of the Scout Law. (Courtesy of Steve Silca.)

After the Remembrance Area dedication, many guests took time to view the names of the honorees and to greet friends. The area has become a place of honor as well as a place to reflect. During the year, numerous visitors make a point of viewing the names on the display boards. (Courtesy of Steve Silca.)

Each summer, the Remembrance Area Steering Committee and the members of the Camp Ma-Ka-Ja-Wan staff organize and conduct a special chapel service to remember and induct the new honorees. The service includes testimonials from those for whom Ma-Ka-Ja-Wan has special meaning. Here, Matt Kasriel, a longtime staff member, gives a testimonial at the dedication service in 2004. (Courtesy of Steve Silca.)

Participants of the Remembrance Area chapel service gather to hear the reading of the names of the 2004 honorees. Matt Horbal and Adam Wilson, Aquatics directors that summer, read the names of each honoree. The roll call was followed by a moment of silence for the honorees. Keven Hansen, Camp Ma-Ka-Ja-Wan administrator (left), led the inaugural service. (Courtesy of Steve Silca.)

The Remembrance Area continues to be a place of honor and reflection. Since its dedication, over 200 names have been added to the plaques. Each name is placed in chronological order and is grouped with the names from each year. The chronological placement emphasizes that no name is more important than the other. (Courtesy of Matt Horbal.)

In 2011, a plan was developed by Mike Landgraf, the original architect of the area, for its expansion to accommodate additional honorees. This plan includes an additional display board and plaque, a statue of the Unknown Scout, and a new sitting area, in addition to a wood canopy. It is the hope of the Remembrance Area Steering Committee that the area continues to be enjoyed by future generations. (Courtesy of Matt Horbal.)

Nine

Camp Staff

Ian Hopkins

In its over 84 years in operation, Camp Ma-Ka-Ja-Wan has had more than a thousand staff members with diverse backgrounds from different areas of the country. For the most part, the staff comes from within the boundaries of the council, as Scouts from troops who attend camp are frequently recruited. The staff has included professional Scouters, adult leaders, Scouts, and residents of the Pickerel and Pearson areas.

The first camp director, Carl McManus, was the assistant scout executive for the North Shore Area Council, BSA. He was appointed by Scout Executive Walter MacPeek.

The camp staff in the early years was responsible for operating a primitive summer camp. The positions on the staff included village or campsite leaders, kitchen staff, Scoutcraft counselors, Aquatics staff, Handicraft staff, a camp ranger, Shooting Sports staff, barge tenders, and nature counselors.

As the years passed, the camp staff was expanded due to the increasing number of campers and the opening of West Camp. In the early 1970s, the addition of the Triangle M Ranch and High Adventure program necessitated the hiring of staff skilled in these areas. Recent additions to the camp program, like dedicated Trailblazer areas, Pinnacle, and Buckskin have further swelled the staff's numbers to well over 100.

Working on the Ma-Ka-Ja-Wan staff is often a very memorable experience and frequently forges lifelong friendships and lifelong involvement with camp. While in the past, few staff members worked more than two or three summers, the number of staff with more than five, or even ten years of service, has been growing, improving the program with an increasing depth of experience.

Every year, each camp staff takes a group photograph. Over the last 15 years, a group of volunteers, including the authors, have collected staff photographs from Camp Ma-Ka-Ja-Wan. This collection includes images of East Camp, West Camp, Reservation, and entire camp staff photographs. East and West Camp staff photographs hang in their respective offices. The 1941 staff photograph shown here was taken in front of the East Camp dining hall.

J. O'Connor was director for Camp Ma-Ka-Ja-Wan in 1932. He is pictured here standing on the shores of Spring Lake in the East Camp Aquatics area. In the early years, this area included a swimming area, rowboats, canoes, and sailboats.

Bill Fox, one of the early village leaders, is seen here in 1948. He served on the camp staff in the 1940s. His brother Jack was one of the first campers at Ma-Ka-Ja-Wan. Both continue to participate with the Boy Scouts as board members for the Northeast Illinois Council. (Courtesy of Dick Behan.)

Dick Miller, from Libertyville, Illinois, sits on the porch of an East Camp staff cabin in the late 1940s. There were three similar cabins, called Last Resort, Z-Hole, and Casbah, located near today's East Staff Row, up the hill behind the Order of the Arrow Lodge. These cabins were removed in the early 1990s for the construction of the current bungalows. (Courtesy of Dick Behan.)

Dick Behan, from Libertyville, Illinois, was an assistant Shawnee Village leader in 1948. At that time, the villages were headed up by a village leader and an assistant village leader. The east villages, later campsites, were initially located much closer to the dining hall than their present locations. Many of their former locations are currently marked with white posts. (Courtesy of Dick Behan.)

In the East Camp dining hall in the early 1950s, Assistant Cook Theora Bazille serves a Boy Scout during a meal. Many Pearson and Pickerel, Wisconsin, families have served on the camp staff. Those families include Powell, Dalton, Skidmore, Thorn, Clark, and Girtz.

In the late 1940s, staff member Tom Tucker conducts a church service for the Boy Scouts and adult leaders. Every Sunday, the camp provided a church service, including Catholic Mass, Jewish services, and Protestant services. The original chapel was replaced by the present one, located at the south end of Spring Lake. (Courtesy of Dick Behan.)

The 1952 East Camp staff photograph was taken in the Firebowl. The East Camp Firebowl, built on the shores of Spring Lake, is used for opening and closing campfires. As today, campfires were designed to entertain the Boy Scouts and adult leaders.

Arvilla Thorn (left) and Ruby Dalton, in the West Camp dining hall kitchen, cook breakfast for the Boy Scouts, adult leaders, and staff members. Both ladies were Pearson residents. According to Dalton, they used to arrive in the camp early in the morning to start breakfast, and they returned home after dinner had been served. Both served on the staff for many years.

Due to canvas shortages in World War II, campsite cabins were constructed to house Scouts. The one shown here, the last such cabin, stood at East Handicraft. It was removed in the mid-1990s. Before the wall tents in use today, Scouts stayed in two-man Voyager tents.

The 1958 camp staff (shown here) was the last staff of the original camp. The staff is posing in the parade field of the day, now called the Dustbowl. The unpainted East Camp trading post and quartermaster building can be seen in the background. Recently remodeled to expand its offerings, this building remains in use today.

Reservation Director Chuck Gribble (left) and 1957 Ma-Ka-Ja-Wan Lodge No. 40 chief Don Verbeke (right) are transported across Spring Lake by Dick Siebel. Behind them is what will become West Waterfront. Gribble was a powerful figure in the camp's history, and his accomplishments include finding and developing the Order of the Arrow Bowl in use today. (Courtesy of Don Verbeke.)

Staff members are dressed up for a meal in the East Camp dining hall in 1948. Harold Thorn is second from left, and Chuck Gribble is at far right. One of the most memorable dining hall programs is the Kangaroo Court, a mock court session when staff members are charged with bogus offenses. The punishment is always to be thrown in the lake, uniform and all. (Courtesy of the Thorn family.)

Staff and Scouts are seen here in the East Camp dining hall. The staff leads dining hall programs during every meal. This includes giving important messages about programs and events in camp, as well as leading camp songs. The staff eat with the campers to provide a more personal experience.

Dave Park (right) served as the reservation director for Ma-Ka-Ja-Wan from 1967 to 1969. He served as program director for the North Shore Area Council and was assigned to run the council's summer camp. In the past five years, he returned to visit Ma-Ka-Ja-Wan to see the camp that he served earlier in his life and to rekindle old relationships.

The 1963 East Camp staff photograph was taken at the camp's entrance. The reservation director, Dan Milzner (first row, center), served during the 1962 and 1963 seasons. The reservation director oversees both camp directors as well as reservation-level programs, food service, maintenance, and overall operations.

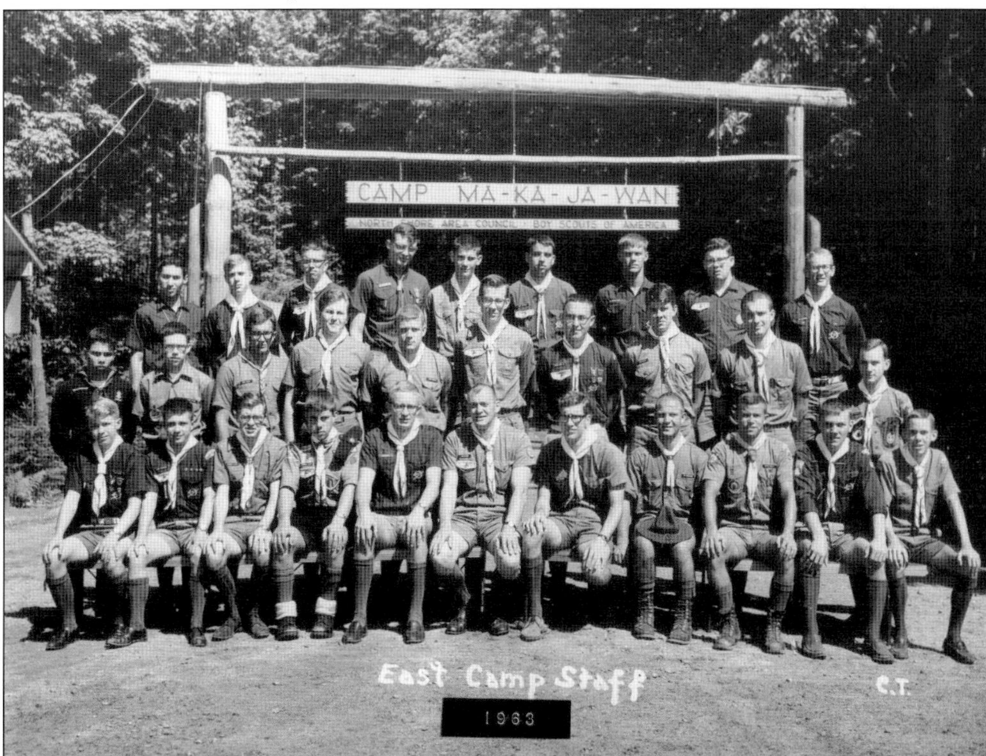

Many Scouts and adult leaders enjoy fishing the waters of Spring Lake. Here, a Scout shows off a fish from a cedar tree extending over the lake. This tree, which recently fell, stood for decades along the trail from the East Firebowl to East Aquatics.

At the Shooting Sports area in West Camp, Tom Monahan takes aim at a target on the archery range. He instructed Boy Scouts in archery while on the Ma-Ka-Ja-Wan staff. Later in his life, he became caretaker for Camp Dan Beard in Wheeling, Illinois, and was a member of the Wilderness Engineering Society, to which he contributed his carpentry skills.

Part of a day in the life of camp administrator, as the reservation director used to be known, is to assist with the Order of the Arrow service projects. In this case, Jim Chandler (center) assists with work on the East Camp Firebowl retaining wall. The Order of the Arrow service projects provide work throughout camp and help to open the camp every spring during the Memorial Day Conclave. (Courtesy of Hank Jostock.)

The 1973 reservation staff was led by Jim Chandler (second row, far left). He brought a commitment to the Scout program and a strong belief in the outdoor experience. His reservation staff was an experienced group. It included Camp Ranger Bob King (third row, third from left), East Camp director Bob Brown (second row, third from right), and West Camp director Al Schirmacher (third row, third from right), among others.

John Buckingham, member of the 1971 East Camp staff, teaches a Boy Scout knots to assist in his rank advancement. Working in the Scoutcraft area, Buckingham taught cooking, camping, hiking, pioneering, wilderness survival, and other outdoor skills. He also served as the Ma-Ka-Ja-Wan lodge chief in 1971.

In 1973, Patricia and Peter Cooper were married at the camp chapel. Camp Ranger Robert G. King served as the best man. Peter Cooper, a Pearson resident, was on the ranger staff. His mother, Pat, was a camp cook in the late 1970s. After leaving camp, Cooper joined the US Army and recently retired as a colonel.

From left to right, Bob King, Harold Schirmer, and Jackie Swanson stand at the Wabaningo entrance gate. King had a long tenure at Ma-Ka-Ja-Wan, serving as both the camp ranger and reservation director. He is credited with starting the High Adventure program and Triangle M Ranch. He also brought and retained many staff members to Ma-Ka-Ja-Wan, many of whom are still actively supporting the camp. (Courtesy of Steve King.)

In 1978, Jim Sanders (left) and Steve Davis served on the West Camp staff. Sanders was the trading post manager and always had a contest or promotion going on for the Boy Scouts. Davis was the quartermaster, in charge of dispersing equipment to troops in camp. Some of that equipment included rakes, shovels, Dutch ovens, and axes. (Courtesy of Steve King.)

In the parade ground, also known as the Dustbowl, East Camp staff members participate in a flag ceremony. They are, from left to right, Ken Soren, Andy Nielsen, Tom Funk, and Mark Gaines. Flag ceremonies are run by the staff and take place before breakfast and dinner every day. In recent times, a cannon is sounded during the ceremonies as a salute. (Courtesy of Bob King.)

On the loading dock of the East Camp dining hall, kitchen staff members gather for a group photograph. Under the leadership of Camp Cook Kris Kyle (back), the kitchen staff members are, from left to right, John Younts, Phil Gormley, Mark Gaines, Mike Pawlowski, and Jim Swanson. They provide meals for hundreds of Boy Scouts, adult leaders, and staff members every day. (Courtesy of Steve King.)

Don "Swanie" Swanson (right) and A.J. Roddenbush stand in the West Camp Field. Swanson was the 1978 West Camp director and served on the staff from 1976 to 1979. Several of Swanson's family members worked on the staff, including his wife Jackie, sons Michael and Jim, and daughter Barbara. He continues to be an active member of the Wilderness Engineering Society and Northeast Illinois Council Executive Boards. (Courtesy of Bob King.)

Eric Jensen, seen here in the West Camp dining hall, joined the Ma-Ka-Ja-Wan staff in 1975 as Aquatics director. He brought along his wife, Phyllis, and two young children. Jensen led his Aquatics staff of three with a wide variety of skills and made physical improvements at West Aquatics. After service as Aquatics director for many years, he brought his leadership to the position of East Camp director in 1981.

The 1983 camp staff poses on the loading ramp to the upper barn in Wabaningo. The staff was led by reservation director Bob King (third row, far left). During that year, the camp earned an "A" rating by the national inspection team for running a quality program and operation. Every year, camp is visited by an accreditation team, and it prides itself on earning perfect marks.

Ernie Garner (left) and John Hopkins converse in front of the gatehouse. At this time, the gatehouse was used as the administration building. Garner, a longtime adult leader from Highland Park, Illinois, joined the staff as business manager in 1984 and became the reservation director in 1985. His daughter Angelique served on the staff of the Triangle M Ranch in 1979 and 1980.

East Camp Eco-Con director Steve King conducts a nondenominational chapel service for Boy Scouts and adult leaders who attended summer camp in the early 1980s. It was fitting that King led such services, as he was a student of the Moody Bible Institute in Chicago at the time. The chapel is still used for weekly services and annual Remembrance Area chapel services.

In the summer of 1980, the camp staff from the east and west side of the lake needed to blow off some steam, so a mock battle broke out, featuring flour bombs and water balloons. The Battle of Sherwood Forest broke out behind the East Camp dining hall. Afterward, everyone sat down together and had a great laugh. This photograph shows the veterans of that battle.

Camp Ma-Ka-Ja-Wan has hosted many international Scouts, including Scouts from the United Kingdom, Israel, and China. One such international scout, Filippo Pezzatti from Switzerland, is seen here, second from the right. He worked on the Scoutcraft staff and was proficient in pioneering. He built many projects that summer as he taught the Pioneering merit badge.

Each week starts with the arrival of new Boy Scouts and adult leaders. After lunch on Sunday, the staff meets in the camp office to fine-tune their plans for the coming week. Many Scouts arrive to the West Camp Field by bus. In this photograph from the late 1970s, staff member John Roe (center) is coordinating the unloading process.

In the early 1980s, registered nurse Ruth LaChance served as a volunteer health lodge director. LaChance, a Troop Committee member from Lake Villa, Illinois, was one of the first women inducted into Ma-Ka-Ja-Wan Lodge No. 40. Her son Keith served on the West Aquatics staff for many years, returning after college as the East Aquatics director.

The 1988 West Camp staff was led by director John Kyle (second row, far right). Kyle was on staff for many years in different positions, including provisional scoutmaster, Aquatics director, High Adventure director, and counselor-in-training coordinator. Currently a scoutmaster of Troop 12 of Oconomowoc, Wisconsin, he brings his troop to Ma-Ka-Ja-Wan every year. Keven Hansen (second row, far left) is seen here in one of his early years on staff.

In one of only a few indoor staff photographs, the 1991 East Camp staff is pictured in front of the East Camp dining hall fireplace. Built in the spring of 1929, the dining hall has remained in service as long as Ma-Ka-Ja-Wan has existed. The dining hall houses many historic items, including the lantern at right on the mantle, which legend says was carried by Ben Pearson in the Ma-Ka-Ja-Wan Bear story.

Bill Crawford (left) and Matt Gummersall pose in front of the West Camp office in 1995. Both were staff members for many years and active within the Order of the Arrow, including time as OA rangers. They are both active in the Wilderness Engineering Society. (Courtesy of Matt Gummersall.)

Claudia Clark has served on the Ma-Ka-Ja-Wan staff for 20 years. She started as East Camp cook in 1994. In 1997, she became the commissary director, serving in that role ever since. Under her leadership, the dining halls on both sides of the lake provide meals to the campers, leaders, and staff. She assists in the off-season with meals for Wilderness Engineering Society weekends.

Keven Hansen, one of Ma-Ka-Ja-Wan's longest-serving staff members, worked a nearly uninterrupted streak from 1985 through 2010. He finished his career as the reservation director from 2002 to 2010 and is one of the few to have served as director for both East and West Camps. His tenure saw many improvements and continued growth. (Courtesy of Matt Horbal.)

Posing on the west side of the East Camp dining hall are, from left to right, Greg Gilpin, Mike Landgraf, Peter Kupfer, and Jim Raup. They are seen here following a flag ceremony. Each worked for several years on the Ma-Ka-Ja-Wan staff. Kupfer was the East Camp director in 2002 and 2003. Landgraf is the designer of the Remembrance Area.

Maintenance workers Bud McBain (left), Marv Fischer (center), and Dan Berg take a break in the back room of the West Camp dining hall. Each gentleman is from the local area and has spent several years on the Ma-Ka-Ja-Wan staff, working closely with the camp ranger to maintain the facilities.

Peter Alonzi (left), the 2002 lodge chief, and Rick Kuzmanoff, the 2004 lodge chief, stand in the West Camp Field. The camp office is seen in the background. Alonzi is serving as an Example, and Kuzmanoff is going for the Brotherhood Honor, during an Order of the Arrow weekend in 2001.

The staff is introduced during the first dinner of the week on Sunday evening. Here, Steve Silca introduces his 2001 Aquatics staff. Silca went on to become the West Camp director from 2002 to 2004. He continues to serve the camp and has become an important figure in the Wilderness Engineering Society, using his skills to improve the camp.

The 2003 West Camp staff is pictured in front of the administration building. Functioning as the base of operations, the building houses a residence in addition to offices for the reservation director, business manager, and High Adventure staff. It is also the first building many visitors to camp enter.

Throughout the years, the staff has expanded in size. This 2010 staff photograph features 95 members. The growth in staff has been necessary to add new program areas, increase supervision ratios to maintain a safe program, and accommodate increasing numbers of Scouts and adult leaders.

One of the highlights of many Scouts' stay at Ma-Ka-Ja-Wan is the climbing wall area in the West Camp Field. Pictured here in 2004 are climbing wall staff members Nicole Gil and Phil Kaehler. They taught the Climbing merit badge and offered open climbs. (Courtesy of Steve Silca.)

Every July 25, the camp celebrates Christmas in July. The staff members gather in the dining hall and exchange humorous and often memorable gifts. Here, John Barkhausen receives his gift. Barkhausen went on to serve as West Camp director in 2010 and 2011. From left to right are Matt Ludmer, Barkhausen, Brian Buesing, Andrew Gern, and Brian Snider. (Courtesy of Matt Horbal.)

One of the most popular program areas in West Camp is Scoutcraft. The 2004 West Scoutcraft staff, shown here from left to right, included Steve Pinkowski, Danny Clarke, George Coyne, Brian Schatz, Chris Alonzi, and Jack Morrison. That summer, the area was located in the pine forest, which was planted shortly before West Camp opened. Schatz went on to become the West Camp director in 2006 and 2007. (Courtesy of Steve Silca.)

One of the traditions at Camp Ma-Ka-Ja-Wan is the use of a small cannon at formal flag-raising and flag-lowering ceremonies. The firing of cannons at formal retreats began in the late 1970s. Shown here celebrating the Fourth of July 2005 with a black-powder salute are, from left to right, Nicole Gil, Kevin Baldwin, John Barkhausen, and Paul Koehring. (Courtesy of Matt Horbal.)

Seen here during a 2005 campfire in the West Camp Firebowl are, from left to right, Brian Buesing, Will Schaeffer, Eric Lillstrom, and Mike Schaeffer. They are performing a skit for Scouts and leaders. Each week kicks off with a campfire put on by the staff. Every program area performs a skit or song. Will Schaeffer went on to serve as the 2006 lodge chief. (Courtesy of Matt Horbal.)

Joe Lepper, East Camp director, leads the staff in song at the end of a campfire in the West Camp Firebowl. At the end of every campfire, the staff sings songs such as "Scout Vespers" and "Land of the Silver Birch" as the campers quietly leave the Firebowl and return to their sites. (Courtesy of Matt Horbal.)

Brian Rasmussen has served on the staff for many years. Starting as the East Camp director in 1995, he now serves as business manager, handling finances, payroll, and purchasing. In this position, he is number two in command and handles affairs when the reservation director is not available. (Courtesy of Matt Horbal.)

Today, the Ma-Ka-Ja-Wan staff continues to expand and provide a quality outdoor experience for all campers who attend summer camp. Since 2011, Jim Neubaum (second row, far left) has served as the reservation director. Due to his leadership and the staff's commitment, Camp Ma-Ka-Ja-Wan continues to be Northeast Illinois Council's premier program offering.

Ten

CAMP MA-KA-JA-WAN TODAY

Matt Horbal, Introduction by Eleesa Kline

Embarking on its 85th year in 2014, Camp Ma-Ka-Ja-Wan is going as strong as ever. Since the camp's dedication in the summer of 1929, it has become an integral part of the outdoor program of the Northeast Illinois Council. According to Ambrose Cantagallo, the vision of the Steering Committee was to find a place for a summer camp that would be used to teach outdoor skills and self-reliance. In the ensuing decades, the leaders of Ma-Ka-Ja-Wan have never wavered from that vision.

To continue what the founding fathers of Camp Ma-Ka-Ja-Wan started, many individuals have strived to add new programs, increase the acreage of the camp, make the camp available and accessible to many more young people and adult leaders, and make it one of the premier summer camps in the Central Region of the Boy Scouts of America.

The staff and leadership of Camp Ma-Ka-Ja-Wan continue to add programs, merit badges, and program areas to broaden and enrich the experiences of the Scouts who spend a week or two in the Northwoods.

One of the new program areas at Ma-Ka-Ja-Wan, Buckskin, is located on the south end of Lake Killian. The creation of longtime staff member John Lillstrom, the area offers Scouts the chance to step back into pioneer times. At Buckskin, Scouts can try tomahawk throwing, taste bear meat, or cool off in their teepee. (Courtesy of John Lillstrom.)

Located near the Buckskin area on the south end of Lake Killian is the Black Hole. This side-by-side slide down a steep hill spits campers out at over 40 miles per hour. Constructed by members of the Wilderness Engineering Society, this slide provides a unique thrill and the opportunity to race friends. (Courtesy of Matt Horbal.)

Pinnacle, another new program area at Ma-Ka-Ja-Wan, provides an area aimed at older Scouts, giving them something new to keep coming back for every year. At locations near East Handicraft (above) and the climbing wall at West Pinnacle (right), the badges offered by these areas are reserved for Scouts ages 13 and older or who have earned the Star rank. East Pinnacle is focused on science and technology badges, while West Pinnacle is focused on fitness and safety. Scouts from both camps are welcome to travel around or across the lake to attend Pinnacle programs in either camp. (Above, courtesy of Austin Coolidge; right, courtesy of Matt Horbal.)

Scouts learn safe and accurate use of .22-caliber rifles on the West Shooting Sports rifle range. Each Shooting Sports area offers Shotgun Shooting, Rifle Shooting, and Archery merit badges as well as open range time. Black-powder demonstrations have also been a part of Shooting Sports programs. (Courtesy of Matt Horbal.)

The East Shooting Sports range, originally constructed at this location by the Wilderness Engineering Society in the 1970s, recently underwent a large expansion and upgrade of facilities, including several new structures and the clearing of several acres of land to better manage noise and safety. Mark Hobson and Kevin Baldwin have spearheaded this project. (Courtesy of Kevin Baldwin.)

New camper shower houses have recently been installed at West Camp (above) and East Camp (below). Boy Scout national standards require a specific number of showers per individuals in camp. With expanding numbers, the older facilities had to be upgraded and replaced. Each shower house offers a number of individual stalls, providing privacy to Scouts and to male and female adult leaders. (Courtesy of Matt Horbal.)

The Ma-Ka-Ja-Wan Trailblazer program offers specialized teaching to first-year Scouts to help them with rank advancement and targeting requirements of the Tenderfoot, Second Class, and First Class ranks. Located near Scoutcraft in West Camp (left) and East Camp (below), each has a dedicated staff prepared to teach the scouts. A new shelter, constructed by the Wilderness Engineering Society, is visible in the below photograph of the East Trailblazer area, where Zach Tipton (left) and Russell Redding (center) teach scouts. At left, Bradley Berg teaches at West Trailblazer. (Left, courtesy of Matt Horbal; below, courtesy of Austin Coolidge.)

Handicraft, one of the traditional program areas at camp, has seen large expansions to its program over the years. As recently as the early 2000s, the area only offered three merit badges, in Leatherwork, Basketry, and Wood Carving. In recent years, with an expanded staff and facilities, Art, Composite Materials, Metalwork, Photography, Pottery, and Space Exploration have been added to its offerings. At right, a Scout works on hammering a metal bowl in a mold. Below, Nick Pellar (left, standing) and Connor Ciesil (right, standing) provide instruction. (Right, courtesy of Matt Horbal; below, courtesy of Austin Coolidge.)

The Eco-Con areas have recently undergone significant upgrades and expansion. Above, staff member Mike Warren teaches Scouts. The recent expansion, more than doubling the size of the original shelter, can be seen in the distance. Below, Jojo Amdur (right) teaches a Scout in the newly renovated East Eco-Con. The renovation also included expanding the existing porch. The East Eco-Con area is located along the shore of Lake Killian and has a dock where Scouts can fish or just take in the views. (Above, courtesy of Matt Horbal; below, courtesy of Austin Coolidge.)

Pioneering projects at Scoutcraft areas, both east and west, are one of the most traditional Scouting pursuits. With every week of Pioneering merit badge, Scouts increase the number and size of the projects in both areas. Each Scoutcraft area provides instruction in outdoor skills, from starting fires and tying knots to orienteering and wilderness survival. At right, staff members Chase Bailey (left) and Collin Anderson work on and enjoy an inverted tripod tower at West Scoutcraft. A large monkey bridge at East Scoutcraft is shown below. In 2013, East Scoutcraft was located in the former location of Shawnee Village, above East Aquatics. (Courtesy of Matt Horbal.)

The Aquatics areas of East and West Camp are among those most enjoyed in camp. Offerings at each Aquatics area include swimming, lifesaving, canoeing, rowing, small-boat sailing, kayaking, motor boating, and, new in 2013, stand-up paddleboarding. Camp Ma-Ka-Ja-Wan is lucky to completely surround Lake Killian, which is a refuge for a family of loons and for a bald eagle living in a tall pine tree above the north end. Above, one of Ma-Ka-Ja-Wan's two matched war canoes participates in a race. Each wooden Old Town war canoe, originally built decades ago and subsequently sheathed in fiberglass, have carried many troops to victory in the weekly Killian Cup. (Above, courtesy of Matt Horbal; below, courtesy of Austin Coolidge.)

The climbing wall in the West Camp Field is one of Ma-Ka-Ja-Wan's High Adventure offerings. Staff, including Barrett Wood (right), provide instructions to Scouts and adults. The wall also offers open climb and a bouldering wall. (Courtesy of Matt Horbal.)

The Triangle M Ranch, located in Wabaningo, was started under the leadership of Bob King. It continues to offer trail rides and the Horsemanship merit badge to Scouts. Alison Geiger, ranch staff, moves the horses from the large front pasture along County Highway T to the smaller back pasture. (Courtesy of Matt Horbal.)

The Wilderness Engineering Society has upgraded and expanded the trading posts in both and East and West Camps in recent years. Both structures used to have a breezeway dividing the quartermaster from the trading post; now the breezeways are enclosed, significantly expanding the trading post. In addition to a broader selection of merchandise, tables for Scouts to socialize and activities like foosball allow them to enjoy a break from merit badge work as well as a snack. The quartermasters, attached to each trading post, continue to serve a vital role, stockpiling tools (rakes and shovels), cooking equipment (Dutch ovens), and other supplies to support each camp. Above, Joe Burson (left) provides help to a Scout. (Courtesy of Austin Coolidge.)

A recent addition to the camp program is an annual Fourth of July parade. Traditionally a smaller week of campers, second period hosts Cub Scout Resident Camp in East Camp and a regular Boy Scout program in West Camp. To make this week extra special, staff decorate camp and personal vehicles to make a number of floats. Cub Scouts come around the lake, and West Camp Scouts line the road through the West Camp Field. Above, Josh Pataky and David Thiel stand at left in the truck bed, with Nick Black on the right, while Sam Gartzman drives. Below, the grand marshal golf cart, driven by Brian Rasmussen, has Don Swanson riding in the passenger seat, with Bud McBain waving a flag from the backseat. (Courtesy of Austin Coolidge.)

Serving on the Ma-Ka-Ja-Wan staff continues to be the highlight of many Scouts' experience at Ma-Ka-Ja-Wan. Pictured here is the 2013 West Aquatics staff, showing off the area's new stand-up paddleboards. Clay Weber (standing, far left) poses next to Aquatics director Max Tuten. Those seated are, from left to right, Christian Hobson, Danny Newhall, Max Auerbach, Brett Towle, Justin Dunn, Jesse Tuten, and Mike Warren. Of note, three are sons of past staff members. (Courtesy of Matt Horbal.)

The Order of the Arrow Callout Ceremony continues to be a highlight of the summer program. Each summer, at three fires at the end of the odd weeks, new members are inducted into the Order of the Arrow. Pictured here is the feather dance during the third fire in 2013. (Courtesy of Matt Horbal.)

Above, 113 members of the 2013 Ma-Ka-Ja-Wan Scout Reservation pose for a staff photograph during Junior Staff Week, before the arrival of Scouts and a summer of teaching, learning, and fun. As it has for the past 84 years, Ma-Ka-Ja-Wan has benefited from the dedication of its staff, Scouts, and adult leaders, all of whom have helped it to become the camp it is today. Members of the Wilderness Engineering Society, Ma-Ka-Ja-Wan Alumni Association, Sea Scout Ship 129, and others continue to dedicate time, monies, and expertise to maintain, improve, and expand Camp Ma-Ka-Ja-Wan so it can continue to offer quality, memorable programs to the Scouts of the Northeast Illinois Council and beyond.

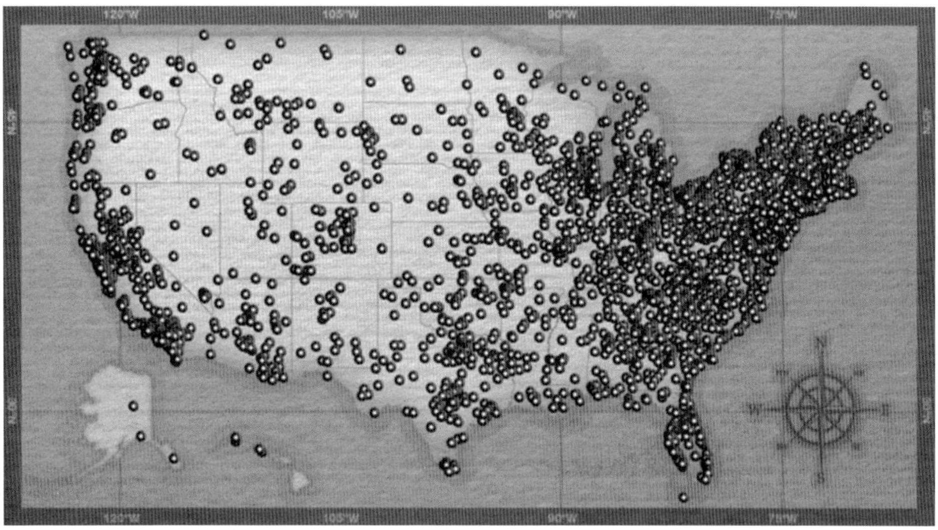

Consistent with our mission to preserve history on a local level, this book was printed in South Carolina on American-made paper and manufactured entirely in the United States. Products carrying the accredited Forest Stewardship Council (FSC) label are printed on 100 percent FSC-certified paper.

MADE IN THE USA